HANDY HEALTH GUIDE
TO YOUR TEETH

Alvin and Virginia Silverstein
and Laura Silverstein Nunn

HANDY HEALTH GUIDES

Enslow Publishers, Inc.
40 Industrial Road
Box 398
Berkeley Heights, NJ 07922
USA

http://www.enslow.com

Original edition published as *Tooth Decay and Cavities* in 1999.

Library of Congress Cataloging-in-Publication Data

Silverstein, Alvin.
Handy health guide to your teeth / by Dr. Alvin Silverstein, Virginia Silverstein, and Laura Silverstein
    Nunn.— First edition.
        pages cm. — (Handy health guides)
  Summary: "An overview of how to care for your teeth and diseases that can affect your mouth"—Provided
by publisher.
Includes bibliographical references and index.
  ISBN 978-0-7660-4280-3
  1. Teeth—Care and hygiene—Juvenile literature. 2. Dental care—Juvenile literature. I. Nunn, Laura Silverstein.
II. Title.
  RK63.S565 2014
  617.6—dc23   2012045288

Future editions:
Paperback ISBN: 978-1-4644-0503-7
EPUB ISBN: 978-1-4645-1260-5
Single-User PDF ISBN: 978-1-4646-1260-2
Multi-User PDF ISBN: 978-0-7660-5892-7

Printed in the United States of America

052013 Lake Book Manufacturing, Inc., Melrose Park, IL

10 9 8 7 6 5 4 3 2 1

To Our Readers: We have done our best to make sure all Internet Addresses in this book were active and appropriate when we went to press. However, the author and the publisher have no control over and assume no liability for the material available on those Internet sites or on other Web sites they may link to. Any comments or suggestions can be sent by e-mail to comments@enslow.com or to the address on the back cover.

Enslow Publishers, Inc., is committed to printing our books on recycled paper. The paper in every book contains 10% to 30% post-consumer waste (PCW). The cover board on the outside of each book contains 100% PCW. Our goal is to do our part to help young people and the environment too!

Illustration Credits: © 2010 Gerald Kelley, www.geraldkelley.com, p. 34; contrail1/Photos.com, p. 32; good eye/ Photos.com, p. 7 (right); Michael Donne/Science Source, p. 41; Nicole diMella, p. 10; Scimat/Science Source, p. 21; Shutterstock.com, pp. 1, 4, 8, 9, 11, 12, 14, 15, 16, 17, 19, 20, 22, 24, 25, 28, 30, 31, 33, 35, 36, 38, 39 (left), 40, 42; Scimat/Science Source, p. 27; Steve Gschmeissner/Science Source, p. 39 (right); Tom Brakefield/Photos.com, p. 7 (left).

Cover Photo: Shutterstock.com (all images)

CONTENTS

If you take care of your teeth, you can have a healthy smile your whole life.

1

TEETH FOR A LIFETIME

"Say 'Cheese!'" That's what people say when they want to take your picture. You give a big, wide smile for the camera to show that you're happy. And when you smile, you show off a nice set of pearly white teeth.

Your teeth aren't there just to make your smile look good. Teeth have a very important job to do—they chew up the food you eat into little pieces so you can swallow it more easily. Actually, you start to digest the food right in your mouth, while you are chewing it.

To help your teeth do their job, you need to take good care of them. If you do, your teeth can last a lifetime.

2
TEETH TELL TALES

You can tell a lot about an animal by looking at its teeth. For example, some animals eat only plant foods—leaves, roots, fruits, or seeds. Many plant eaters have very good cutting teeth. Their front teeth are large and sharp so they can snip off leaves and stems or bite off roots with ease. A beaver's front teeth are so big and strong that it can even gnaw through tree trunks. Grazing animals such as horses and cows are plant eaters, too. Their large back teeth are good for grinding up leaves or grains.

Some animals eat mainly meat. They hunt other animals for food. Their teeth are very different from those of plant eaters. Dogs, cats, and other meat eaters have long, pointed fangs. They use them to bite into their prey and tear the meat into pieces small enough to swallow. They have cutting and grinding teeth too, but those are not very big or strong. (If you watch a pet cat or dog eating, you may notice that it does not chew its food very well. It just swallows it down in chunks.)

Look at a mirror and check out the inside of your own mouth. Your front teeth are not as strong as a

Meat eaters, such as this gray wolf, use their fangs to tear flesh into pieces that are small enough to swallow.

Plant eaters, such as this beaver, use their large front teeth to gnaw on branches, stems, and roots.

Think of all the different types of food on a slice of pizza—cheese, sausage, pepperoni, mushrooms, onions, peppers, tomatoes. Your teeth can chew them all.

You Are What You Eat

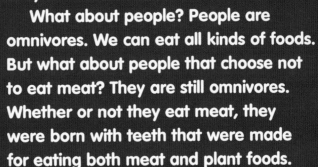

What do you call animals that eat mainly meat? Carnivores. What about animals that eat mainly plants? They are herbivores. Some animals eat both meat and plants. They are called omnivores.

What about people? People are omnivores. We can eat all kinds of foods. But what about people that choose not to eat meat? They are still omnivores. Whether or not they eat meat, they were born with teeth that were made for eating both meat and plant foods.

beaver's cutting teeth, but they are good enough to take a bite out of an apple or a carrot. Your back teeth are not as big or wide as those of a horse, but you can still crunch vegetables and mash them into a soft pulp. And you don't have long fangs like a cat or a dog, but your teeth can handle meat—even a tough piece of steak— pretty well. People eat both plant foods and meat, so you have teeth that are good for chewing many different types of foods.

3

TWO SETS OF TEETH

Babies are born without any teeth showing at all. At first they can drink only liquids like milk, water, or juice. After a few months, they may eat some soft foods like applesauce, ground-up bananas, or mashed peas.

The first teeth, called milk teeth, appear when an infant is about six months old. One by one they pop out of the gums—first the cutting teeth in front, then some grinding teeth and tearing teeth. It takes about two years for all 20 milk teeth to come in.

This baby has no teeth. Her "first teeth" will appear when she is about six months old.

A crocodile can replace lost teeth throughout its life.

When a child is about five or six years old, the milk teeth start to fall out. These "baby teeth" are replaced, one at a time, by larger ones called permanent teeth. There are 32 teeth in a complete set of permanent teeth. These are the teeth that we keep for the rest of our lives.

Why do people grow two sets of teeth? A complete set of permanent teeth can't fit into a baby's tiny mouth. That's why they come later, when a child is a little bigger.

Animals such as cats and dogs have two sets of teeth, just like people do. Reptiles and fish may have many sets of teeth during their lives. Crocodiles and sharks, for example, can keep on replacing their teeth their whole life.

Tooth Trade—Ins

Did the tooth fairy visit your home when you were young? In the United States, when kids lose a baby tooth, they put it under their pillow. When they wake up the next morning, they find that the "tooth fairy" took the tooth and left money in its place. In some other countries, children put their baby teeth where a "tooth mouse" can find them. They hope their new teeth will be as strong and sharp as a mouse's teeth.

This boy is missing a front tooth. You see the permanent tooth just under the surface of the gum.

4

INSIDE YOUR MOUTH

You have several kinds of teeth in your mouth. Each type of tooth has a special job to do. When you look in the mirror and smile, you see two rows of flat, squared-off teeth right in the front of your mouth. There are four on top and four smaller teeth below. These front teeth are called incisors. They are sharp and act like knives to slice and bite off chunks of food. (Look at your "toothprint" after you bite into an apple to see how broad and sharp your teeth are.)

Next to the incisors are teeth called canines. The word "canine" comes from the Latin word for "dog." Canine teeth are pointed like the fangs of a dog. We use our canines to tear food into small pieces. You have four canines, two in the upper jaw and two in the lower jaw.

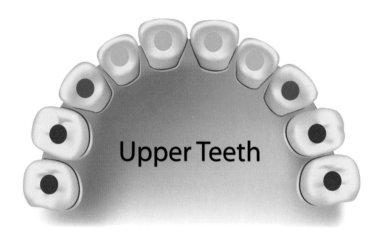

Upper Teeth

MILK TEETH

Lower Teeth

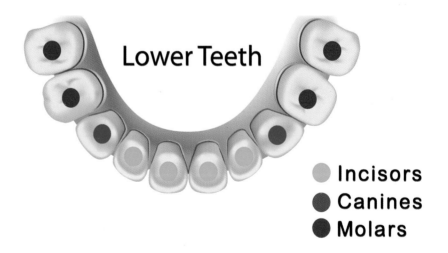

- Incisors
- Canines
- Molars

PERMANENT TEETH

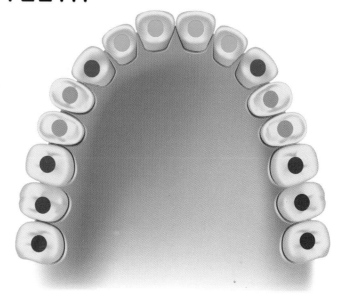

Upper Teeth

- Incisors
- Canines
- Premolars
- Molars

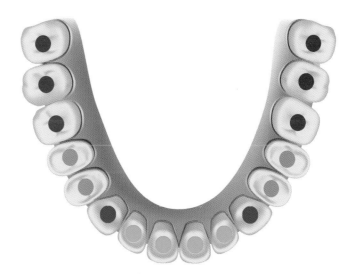

Lower Teeth

Teeth Are Not Tools

Have you ever used your teeth to rip open a bag of potato chips, tear a piece of plastic tape, yank off the tag from a clothing item, or crack open a pistachio nut? We're all guilty of doing at least one of those things at some point. But dentists say that using teeth as tools can result in chipped or broken teeth. Teeth are tools for chewing food, not scissors or pliers. They are strong, but they are not indestructible.

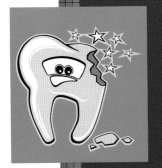

Farther back are the premolars and then the molars. The premolars have two pointed peaks. They look like two canine teeth put together. The molars are broader and have three pointed peaks. Their tops are flat with raised bumps and ridges. They crush and grind food so that you can swallow it easily.

Your teeth are firmly planted in your jaws. Deep inside the upper and lower jaws are jawbones. Long roots grow from the bottom of each tooth, connecting it to your jawbone. Soft pink gums cover the jawbones and help to hold your teeth in place.

Your upper jawbone cannot move. It is actually a part of the skull, the bony case that forms the shape of the head. Your lower jawbone can move up, down, and even sideways. When you move your jaw, you move your teeth. The muscles that control your jaws are powerful, so your teeth can grind food with great force.

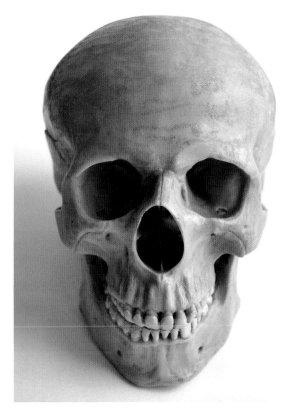

By looking at this human skull, you can see how your teeth are firmly planted in your jawbones.

5

WHAT'S IN A TOOTH?

What are teeth made of? The whitish covering on the teeth is called enamel. It is the hardest substance in your whole body. Only the crown of the tooth (the part you can see) and the neck (the part at the gum line) are covered with enamel. The root is buried deep inside the gum, so it does not need this extra-hard protection.

Under the outer covering of enamel is a hard yellowish substance called dentin. It is actually harder than bone. Most of the tooth is made up of dentin.

The center of each tooth is filled with soft material called pulp. Tiny blood vessels and nerves run through the pulp. The blood vessels bring nutrients to the dentin and help keep it healthy and strong. The nerves

PARTS OF A TOOTH

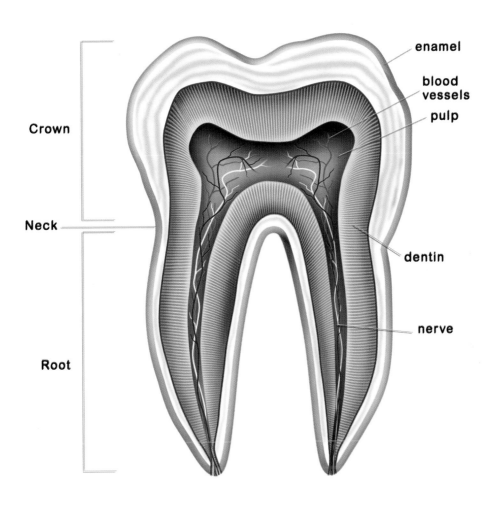

enamel

blood vessels

pulp

dentin

nerve

Crown

Neck

Root

19

inside teeth send messages to the brain, so that you always know what your teeth are doing. You can feel it when you bite into something, and know just how hard you are biting.

Handy Healthy Fact

Are Your Teeth White?

Toothpaste commercials talk about shining white smiles. But not everyone has bright white teeth. The enamel of some people's teeth is naturally slightly yellow, no matter how much they clean their teeth. In fact, the yellowish enamel may be even stronger than the whiter kind. Stains from drinking coffee or tea can also make teeth yellow.

6

THE MICROWORLD IN YOUR MOUTH

Would you believe that there are millions of tiny creatures living inside your body? These creatures, known as bacteria, are so small that you can see them only with a microscope.

Many kinds of bacteria live in our bodies. Some are "good" and some are "bad." "Good" bacteria help us. For instance, bacteria that live in your intestines break down the food you eat so that you can digest it more easily.

If you could look at teeth through a microscope, you would be able to see the bacteria that live there.

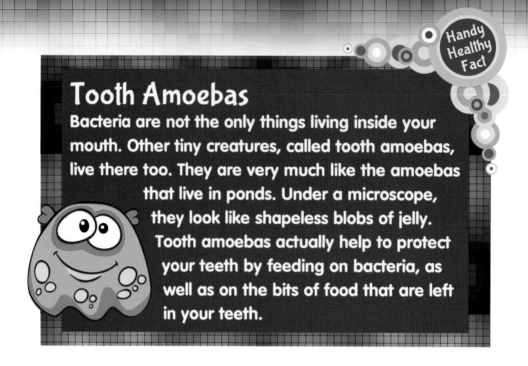

Tooth Amoebas

Bacteria are not the only things living inside your mouth. Other tiny creatures, called tooth amoebas, live there too. They are very much like the amoebas that live in ponds. Under a microscope, they look like shapeless blobs of jelly. Tooth amoebas actually help to protect your teeth by feeding on bacteria, as well as on the bits of food that are left in your teeth.

Some bacteria make us sick. For instance, you may get strep throat because bacteria attack your body and make you ill.

If you could look through a microscope at the inside of your own mouth, you might be shocked at what you saw. A tiny world of bacteria is having a party inside your mouth! At this party, you bring the food and the bacteria just eat. When you eat a hamburger, for example, you chew it up into tiny pieces with your teeth, and then you swallow it. Now the hamburger is gone, right? Well, not exactly. Every time you eat something, tiny bits of food are left on your teeth. Bacteria feed on these little bits of food. And these bacteria are germs that can really harm your teeth.

7

HOW CAVITIES FORM

Millions of bacteria feast on the food left in your teeth. Bacteria grow and multiply, eventually covering your teeth with a soft, sticky coat of plaque. Plaque is a mixture of bits of leftover food, bacteria, and other substances. It forms mainly between the teeth and at the edge of the gums. (With your fingernail, scrape gently along some of your teeth, starting at your gums. Did you scrape off some soft, whitish stuff? That's plaque.)

When you do not clean your teeth regularly, plaque can build up. If left for more than a few days, plaque hardens into tartar, which is more difficult to remove.

As the bacteria grow on your teeth, they make an acid that slowly eats through the tooth enamel.

This is tooth decay. And once it gets through the hard enamel into the softer dentin, that acid works fast. Eventually, tooth decay makes a cavity—a hole in the tooth. Bacteria make even more acid when you eat sugary foods.

You may get cavities no matter how well you take care of your teeth. Studies show that good or bad teeth may be inherited. So you could have strong teeth like

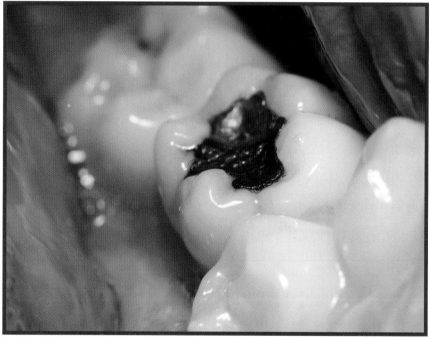

Do your parents have a mouth full of fillings? If so, you might too one day. But brushing with fluoride toothpaste and flossing can help you have a healthier mouth.

Ice pops are usually a treat. But if you have a cavity, eating one can be painful.

one parent—or get a mouth full of cavities like the other parent.

Your teeth may give you some clues to let you know that a cavity is forming. If eating a bowl of hot soup or a cold ice cream cone makes your teeth hurt, you could have a cavity.

When acid from bacteria eats away the tooth enamel and then the dentin, it moves into the pulp. As soon as it comes into contact with a nerve—ouch! You now have a toothache. Toothaches can be very painful and should be checked by a dentist. But not all toothaches are that serious. Sometimes, food gets stuck between teeth. (That often happens with popcorn!) This can bother your gums, and cause your tooth to throb with pain. The good news is that the pain will go away as soon as you floss your teeth and get rid of the food.

Bacteria can also grow down into the gums and cause gum disease. Gum disease usually affects adults. One of the most common types of gum disease is gingivitis, or swelling of the gums.

Your body does not let bacteria take over your mouth without a fight. It has a defense called saliva— the watery stuff that fills your mouth when you eat or sometimes even when you think about food.

Handy Healthy Fact

Activity 1: How Is an Egg Like a Tooth?

You can try to make an eggshell decay, just like a tooth. You'll need a hard-boiled egg and a bowl of vinegar. Let the egg sit in the vinegar for about a day. The vinegar is acidic, just like the acid that the bacteria make in your mouth. When you check on the egg, you'll see that part of the shell has been eaten away by the vinegar. Tooth decay works the same way.

Your mouth makes about a quart of the stuff every day! Saliva is very important. It mixes with your food to make chewing and swallowing easier. Saliva also helps to clean your teeth by washing away food leftovers. It contains chemicals that help cut down the amount of acid made by the bacteria.

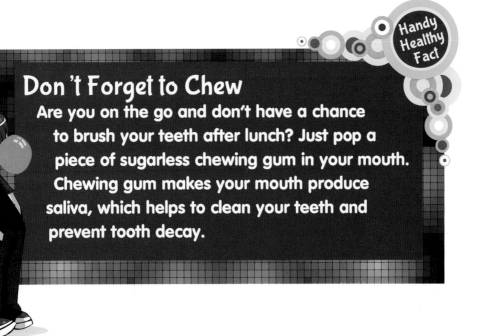

Handy Healthy Fact

Don't Forget to Chew

Are you on the go and don't have a chance to brush your teeth after lunch? Just pop a piece of sugarless chewing gum in your mouth. Chewing gum makes your mouth produce saliva, which helps to clean your teeth and prevent tooth decay.

8

GOING TO THE DENTIST

How often do you go to the dentist? You should have a checkup every six months. This is the best way to keep from getting cavities.

In a routine visit, your teeth get a cleaning that will leave them smooth and healthy. The dental hygienist may begin with an instrument that uses ultrasound to blast away bits of tartar from your teeth. As it works, the device makes a humming or high-pitched

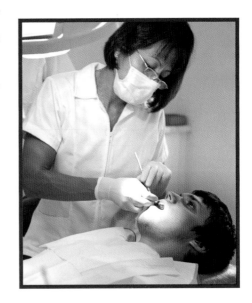

This dentist is checking a patient's teeth for cavities.

28

whistling sound. It has no sharp edges, so it doesn't hurt. But you may feel strong "tickling" vibrations along your teeth and gums.

The dental worker will then switch to a tooth scraper, a curved instrument that scrapes away plaque buildup. It may also pick out bits of food stuck between your teeth. Once the tooth surfaces are all smooth, an electric toothbrush cleans and polishes your teeth. The toothpaste in the dentist office is a little different from the kind you use at home. It feels a little gritty, like sand, which helps to clean and smooth the tooth surfaces.

During the visit, the dentist checks all your teeth, looking for any problems. Holes or cracks in the enamel and dark-colored spots are signs of trouble. But cavities are sometimes hard to spot, especially if they are between teeth or at the edge of gums.

The dentist can find those cavities by taking X-ray pictures of your teeth. X-rays show parts of the teeth and jawbone that are hidden inside the gums. If you are lucky, the X-rays will show that you do not have any cavities. But if you do have cavities, the X-rays will show the dentist exactly where they are.

This dental hygienist is polishing a person's teeth.

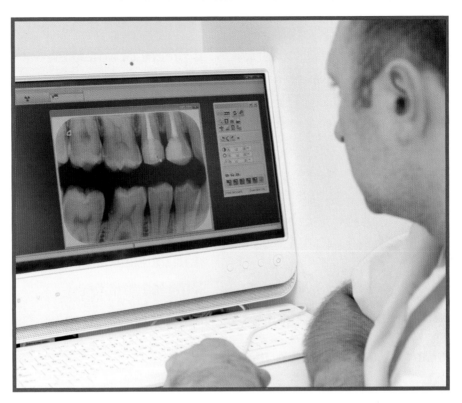

A dentist can look at X-rays of your mouth to check for cavities or other problems with your teeth.

Cavities should be fixed as soon as possible so that tooth decay does not get any worse. To do this, the dentist must put a filling in the cavity. Most fillings are made of amalgam, a mixture of silver, mercury, and other metals. Amalgam fillings are often called "silver" fillings. But some people are worried about the mercury in these fillings. Mercury is dangerous when it gets into

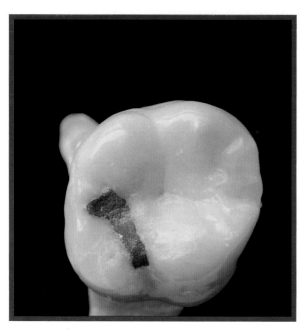

This molar has an amalgam filling.

the body. What happens if pieces of amalgam break off and then get swallowed? Does all the mercury stay in the amalgam, or can it leak out into the body? Actually, health experts don't all agree on whether amalgam fillings harm people. Still, some countries—Austria, Canada, Denmark, Germany, and Sweden—have banned or discouraged the use of amalgam fillings.

In the United States, amalgam is still widely used. However, dentists do offer other alternatives, such as composites, called "white fillings," and porcelain, made of ceramic. They look better than amalgam because they are made with tooth-colored materials.

Filling cavities takes a bit more work than simply putting the filling right in the cavity. Bits of food and bacteria might be hiding there. If they are not removed,

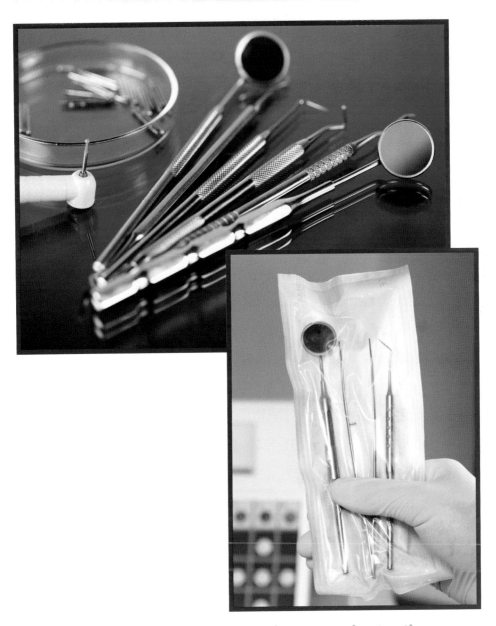

A dentist uses several tools to clean out the tooth decay before filling a cavity.

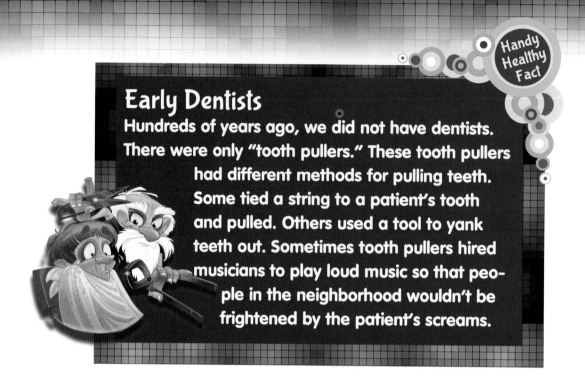

Early Dentists

Hundreds of years ago, we did not have dentists. There were only "tooth pullers." These tooth pullers had different methods for pulling teeth. Some tied a string to a patient's tooth and pulled. Others used a tool to yank teeth out. Sometimes tooth pullers hired musicians to play loud music so that people in the neighborhood wouldn't be frightened by the patient's screams.

the bacteria might continue to grow and multiply, producing more acid and making a bigger hole in your tooth. Dentists use a drill to clean out the hole and get rid of all the bad stuff. (Before the dentist starts to drill, you may be given a shot, or a patch with a pain-killing drug may be placed on your gum. This numbs your mouth so you will not feel any pain.)

Sometimes, a tooth is so badly decayed that it can't be saved. In that case, the dentist may have to extract, or pull out, the tooth. You may be given anesthesia for a tooth extraction, to keep you from feeling any pain. After the tooth is taken out, your gum may feel sore.

Sometimes a badly damaged tooth can be saved by root canal therapy. A root canal is a narrow, hollow tunnel in a tooth's root. When the decay spreads down into the tooth, the pulp may become infected. Then a dentist may treat the infection by performing root canal therapy to take out the pulp. The pulp is replaced with a solid packing material that helps to hold the tooth in place.

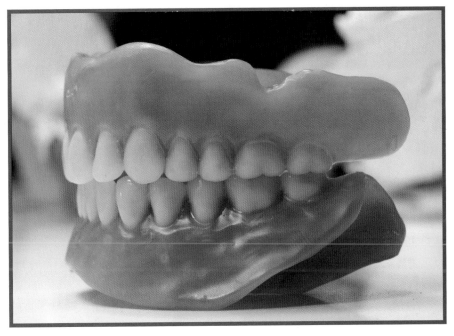

The false teeth in a denture rest in a tough, plastic base that is fitted to the patient's mouth.

What's Your Flavor?

Toothpaste for dental cleanings may come in different flavors, including strawberry, orange, cinnamon, or even chocolate. These flavors may sound good enough to eat, but you're not supposed to eat toothpaste. You should spit it out after you're done brushing. Many toothpastes contain fluoride. Fluoride is good for your teeth because it makes the enamel stronger and prevents tooth decay. But if you eat toothpaste, the fluoride could build up in your body and make you really sick. Don't worry if you accidentally swallow a little when you brush your teeth, though. That's not enough to hurt you.

When accidents happen, a tooth may be chipped, broken, or cracked. As long as the root of the tooth is not damaged, it can probably be saved. One way is by putting a crown, or cap, on it. The crown is cemented right over the damaged tooth. It can look as good and work as well as a normal tooth. If the whole tooth is missing, the dentist may make a bridge. This is a false tooth that is attached to good teeth on either side of the empty space. A missing tooth can also be replaced with an implant—a false tooth that is set into the gum and permanently attached to the jawbone. Implants work like natural teeth. If all of the teeth are missing or have to be taken out, the dentist can make a complete set of false teeth, which is called a denture.

Dentists have many ways to fix teeth, but they'd much rather find no cavities at all when you come in for a checkup. You can help the dentist take care of your teeth by brushing and flossing them regularly at home.

9

HOW TO PREVENT CAVITIES

Brushing and flossing your teeth can make a big difference in preventing tooth decay. Cleaning your teeth does not have to be a chore. If you do it every day, brushing and flossing become a habit, just like taking a shower or combing your hair.

Be sure to use a toothpaste with fluoride in it. Many cities now add fluoride to their drinking water. Thanks to fluoride, children today get far fewer cavities than they did many years ago.

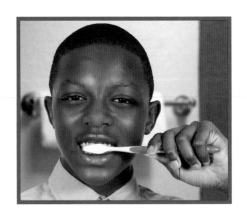

You should brush your teeth after every meal. That's not

Brush at least twice a day to keep your teeth healthy.

always easy—especially if you like to have snacks during the day. But be sure to brush your teeth at least twice a day—when you get up in the morning and before you go to bed. Researchers found that if teeth are cleaned at least once within 24 hours, bacteria cannot make enough acid to damage them.

You should get a new toothbrush about every two to three months. Bacteria can grow in a toothbrush, so you put germs into your mouth when you use it.

You should also floss at least once a day. Bacteria feed on food that is left between your teeth. Moving a

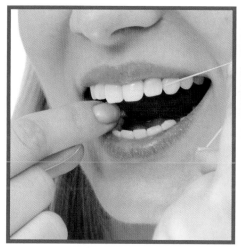

Flossing can remove the bacteria and food particles that brushing misses.

A picture taken through a microscope shows bacteria on a piece of dental floss.

How to Brush Your Teeth

How do you brush your teeth? Here are some general rules for a complete cleaning:

1. Move your toothbrush up and down and in circles.
2. Brush the top teeth downward from the gums.
3. Brush the bottom teeth upward from the gums.
4. Brush the backs and chewing surfaces of all the teeth.
5. Brush for at least two minutes for strong, clean teeth. (The average person brushes for only 45 seconds.)
6. Rinse thoroughly—and smile!

strand of dental floss back and forth between your teeth will remove the bits of food that you missed while you were brushing. Moving the floss up and down between the teeth will help prevent plaque build-up.

What kind of foods do you eat? Do you eat a lot of vegetables and fruits? What about candy? We're told to

Activity 2:
How Clean Are Your Teeth?

You can find out by using disclosing tablets or a special mouthwash that colors the plaque on your teeth with a bright vegetable dye. You can buy the tablets from the drugstore, or your dentist may give you some samples.

Chew a tablet for 30 seconds but do not swallow it. Your teeth will be covered with a bright color, such as red or purple. Wash your mouth out with water. Look at your teeth in a mirror. Where are the darkest color stains? These places show where the plaque buildup is. Now you know where you need to brush your teeth better next time.

stay away from sweets like cookies and candy. But you might be surprised to find out that foods like cornflakes and raisins may be to blame for the holes in your teeth. Starches like potato chips and crackers may not taste sweet, but to bacteria, they're just like lollipops. Saliva breaks starches down into a sugar, called maltose, and bacteria really like maltose. Starches are especially bad for your teeth because they actually stick around longer than sugars do. This gives bacteria more time to cause cavities.

There's an old saying that "Milk does a body good." It's true. Milk, cheese, and green vegetables contain

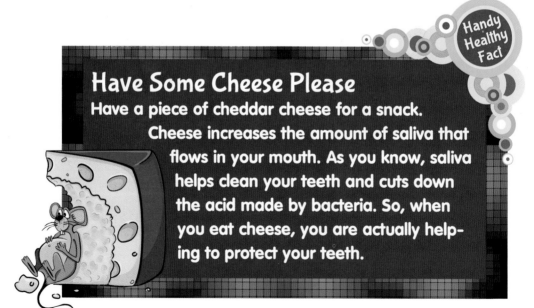

Handy Healthy Fact

Have Some Cheese Please
Have a piece of cheddar cheese for a snack. Cheese increases the amount of saliva that flows in your mouth. As you know, saliva helps clean your teeth and cuts down the acid made by bacteria. So, when you eat cheese, you are actually helping to protect your teeth.

calcium, which helps keep your bones and teeth strong and healthy. Other substances in these foods are also good for your teeth.

If you watch what you eat, brush and floss your teeth after meals, and visit the dentist regularly, you will help make your teeth the best that they can be.

Maybe someday we will live in a world without cavities. It may sound like a fantasy, but scientists have been working on vaccines against tooth-decay bacteria. In 2011, researchers reported on a new vaccine that cuts down the amount of bacteria growing on teeth—and greatly reduces the number of cavities.

Researchers are also working on ways to fix cavities without that painful drilling. For example, they have developed a gel that can be dabbed onto an infected tooth. A chemical in the gel helps rebuild the tooth! Experiments showed that after about a month of treatment, the cavities disappeared.

With all these promising studies, visits to the dentist may be less frequent and much more pleasant in the future.

GLOSSARY

amalgam—A mixture of silver, mercury, and other metals used for filling cavities.

anesthesia—Use of a drug to stop a person from feeling pain.

bridge—One or more false teeth used to replace a missing tooth or teeth. It is attached to the good teeth on each side of the empty space.

canines—Pointed teeth on each side of the incisors. They are used to tear food.

cavity—A hole in a tooth, produced by tooth decay.

composite—White filling; a tooth-colored mixture used for filling cavities.

crown—The top part of a tooth, above the gums. It can also refer to an artificial cap placed over a broken or damaged tooth.

dentin—A hard, yellowish substance that makes up most of a tooth.

denture— A complete set of false teeth that can be removed from the mouth.

enamel—The outer covering of a tooth.

extract—To pull out a tooth.

filling—A substance that a dentist puts into a cavity to stop tooth decay.

fluoride—A mineral that helps to make teeth stronger. It may be added to toothpaste or drinking water or applied to the teeth by a dentist.

gingivitis—Painful swelling of the gums.

gum disease—Damage to the gums caused by trapped food or bacteria.

gums—The soft pink tissue inside the mouth that surrounds the teeth.

implant—A false tooth that is set into the gum and permanently attached to the jawbone.

incisors—Front teeth with a flat, squared-off shape. These teeth are used for cutting food.

jawbones—The bones of the upper and lower jaws, to which the roots of the teeth are attached. Only the lower jawbone can move.

jaws—Bony structures between the nose and the chin that hold the teeth.

milk teeth—A child's first set of teeth.

molars—Broad teeth with three points, the farthest back in the mouth. They crush and grind food.

neck—The middle part of a tooth, at the gum line.

nerve—A structure that carries messages to the brain.

permanent teeth—Teeth that replace the milk teeth.

plaque—A mixture of leftover food, bacteria, and other substances that forms on teeth, especially between teeth and at the edge of the gums.

porcelain—A hard, tooth-colored substance used for filling cavities.

premolars—Teeth with two points, located between the canines and the molars. They can tear and grind food.

pulp—A soft substance that fills the center of a tooth. It contains nerves and blood vessels.

root—The lower part of a tooth, which holds it in the gums and attaches it to the jawbone.

root canal therapy—Replacement of the pulp in the root of a decayed tooth with solid packing material.

tartar—Plaque that has hardened.

tooth amoeba—A microscopic jellylike creature that lives in the gums and feeds on bacteria.

tooth decay—The effects of acid produced by bacteria in the mouth, which eats through the outer layers of a tooth, producing a hole or cavity.

LEARN MORE

Books

Libal, Autumn. *Taking Care of Your Smile: A Teen's Guide to Dental Care*. Broomhall, Pa.: Mason Crest Publishers, 2005.

Macaulay, David, with Richard Walker. *The Way We Work: Getting to Know the Amazing Human Body*. Boston: Houghton Mifflin, 2008.

O'Sullivan, Robyn. *Your 206 Bones, 32 Teeth, and Other Body Math*. Washington, D.C.: National Geographic, 2006.

Walker, Sally M. *Written in Bone: Buried Lives of Jamestown and Colonial Maryland*. Minneapolis: Carolrhoda Books, 2009.

Web Sites

American Dental Association. *ADA for Kids*. © 1995–2013.
<http://www.ada.org/353.aspx>

Nemours. *KidsHealth*. "Taking Care of Your Teeth." © 1995–2013.
<http://kidshealth.org/teen/your_body/take_care/teeth.html>

INDEX